Fundamentals of Freehand
LONGARM
QUILTING™

© ANNIE'S

Terri L. Watson

Table of Contents

Meet Terri L. Watson

Terri came to quilting in 1989 after dabbling in a few other hobbies. Once she started her first quilt she knew she had found a "home."

For the first 15 years or so, she machine-pieced and hand-quilted her projects. When her job as a high-school library supervisor became threatened by budget cuts, she began to research the possibility of making a career out of her love of quilting.

She purchased her Gammill longarm quilting system in December of 2004. She began quilting for others in May of 2005. The quilting has always been her favorite part of the process, and she gets to do it every day.

Terri believes that the quilting is an integral part of the design of a quilt, and it deserves as much attention as the selection of the quilt-top design and the fabrics.

She considers herself to be an "everyday" quilter and works to learn and develop designs that are affordable for her clients and that look terrific on the quilt.

Terri lives in beautiful western Michigan with her husband, Maris. They have one daughter, Aubrey. Many of the quilts Terri has quilted for others have been featured in shows and have won awards.

Introduction

Welcome to your longarm quilting adventure! Wow— that sounds lame, but I am sitting here writing notes for a book and a video class, which is something that I could never have imagined when I started down this path a little over eight years ago. So, adventure it is.

I have been a professional machine quilter for about eight years. I own a Gammill Classic Plus machine. It has a 26-inch throat (the open space between the needle and the back of the machine). The "Plus" means my machine has an electronic stitch regulator that ensures consistent stitch length.

I began making quilts around 1990—piecing by machine and hand-quilting them. In December of 2004, after months of research into machines and the business of quilting for others, my quilting system was delivered. Six months after that, I began to quilt for others—pretty straightforward, right?

Not quite.

The morning after my quilting system was delivered and set up was interesting. That's a good word for it—interesting. I walked downstairs to my studio and saw that big (and expensive) piece of equipment. My heart started pounding in my chest and my stomach dropped. For all of my research, planning and organizing, I was scared. I had made a mistake. What was I thinking? I had taken a very large chunk of our savings and poured it into something that I wasn't even sure I could do. I was thinking a lot of other things as well, but most of them were unintelligible jibberings.

Grabbing my manual and a bolt of wide muslin I began to load a practice piece—three times; seriously, three times. I thought I had followed the instructions step by step, but I kept messing it up. By the third time I was frustrated and near to tears, but I finally got it right. It was noon, and I was exhausted. Half the day was gone and I hadn't even turned the machine on. It was not my best morning.

After a good lunch and some deep breaths I got myself together and headed back to the studio. And I quilted all afternoon. By dinnertime I was tired, but happy. Oh, the quilting I did was awful, but I felt better about my ability to learn this skill.

That leads to my first tip—keep that first practice piece. I got rid of mine somewhere along the way, but I recommend that you keep yours tucked away. When you are having a crummy day quilting you can pull it out and see how far you have come. You will be amazed.

In *The Fundamentals of Freehand Longarm Quilting* I hope to help you get comfortable with your quilting system, show you some different methods for loading and attaching your quilts, sprinkle in some tips to help things go more smoothly, and wind it up with some simple but effective freehand allover designs to get you quilting right now!

Please remember that what I have presented here is not written in stone. There is no one right way. These are things that have worked for me and for many of my students. Keep exploring. Pay attention when you see someone doing something differently. I do, and I learn something new every day. I hope you will too!

Types of Quilting Systems

There are many different types and brands of quilting systems available to quilters today. The choices can be confusing. Since this is a big monetary investment, you should research carefully to find the system that best fits your needs and pocketbook.

Stand-Up Systems

There are several different types of stand-up systems—longarm, midarm and shortarm. Industry standards define these systems by the length of the arm, which is the distance between the needle and the sewing head or the throat. With these systems, you are moving the machine head over the quilt layers to stitch a design.

© GAMMILL QUILTING SYSTEMS

© TINLIZZIE

Longarm Systems

A longarm stand-up system is generally a three-rail quilting system with a throat that measures 18" or more. The quilting area can range from 10" to more than 20". A longarm system includes a table-mounted frame that is 8–14 feet long and requires a large floor space. It can have front and rear handles on the stitching head.

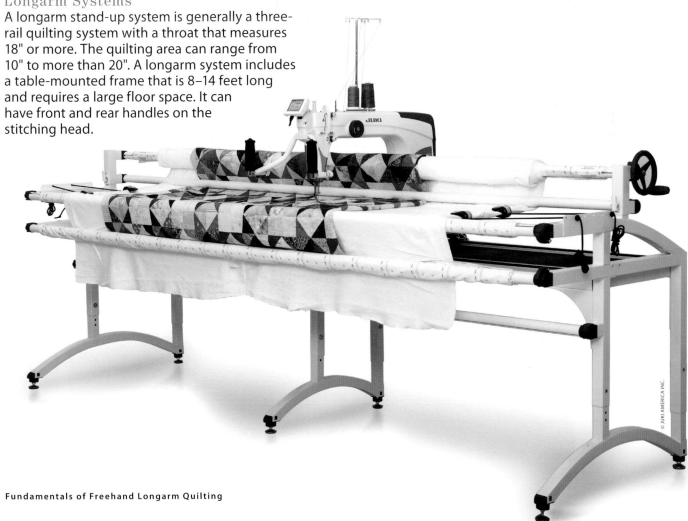

© JUKI AMERICA INC.

8

Midarm Systems

A midarm stand-up system is generally a three-rail quilting system with a throat that measures approximately 12"–18". These machines may be mounted on a table or a frame. Some have both front and rear controls on the stitch head. The rear controls allow the quilter to use pantograph designs rather than depend exclusively on freehand quilting.

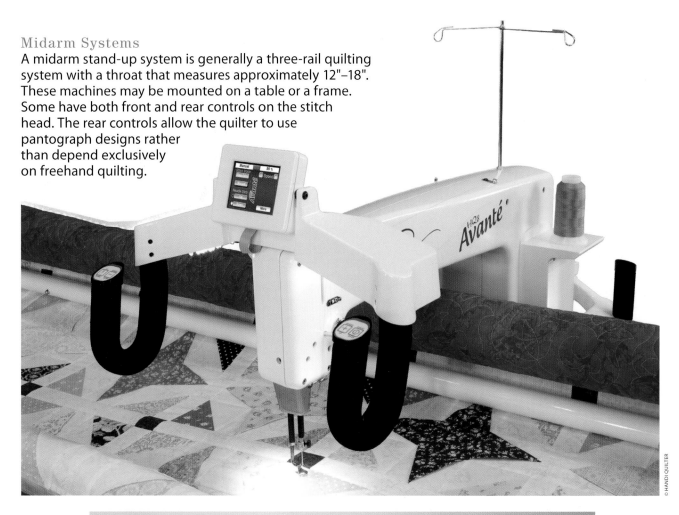

© HANDI QUILTER

© NOLTING MFG.

Shortarm Systems

A shortarm stand-up system is generally a three-rail quilting system with a throat that measures less than 12 inches. This type of system works well in a small space. It uses a smaller, less expensive frame designed for home use.

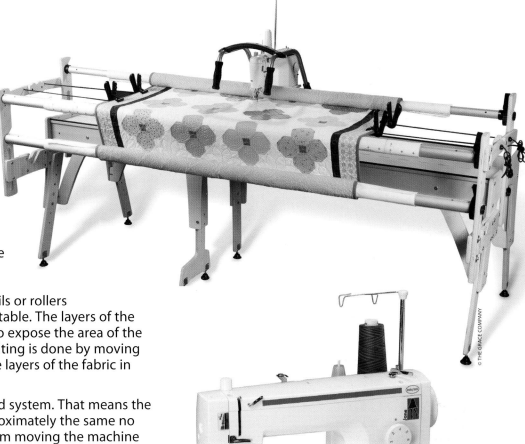

In the previous systems the quilt is "loaded" onto the machine by attaching the layers of the quilt to the rails or rollers that run along the system table. The layers of the quilt sandwich are rolled to expose the area of the quilt to be worked on. Quilting is done by moving the machine head over the layers of the fabric in some kind of pattern.

I work on a stitch-regulated system. That means the stitches per inch stay approximately the same no matter how fast or slow I am moving the machine head. This is helpful for a beginner because the machine will balance the stitch length according to the movement of the machine head to prevent long and short or even skipped stitches.

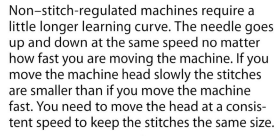

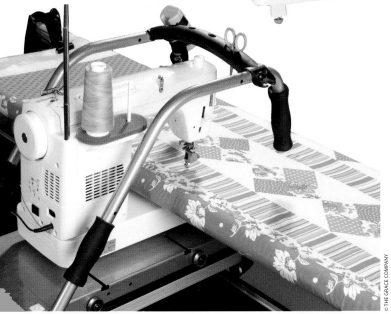

Non–stitch-regulated machines require a little longer learning curve. The needle goes up and down at the same speed no matter how fast you are moving the machine. If you move the machine head slowly the stitches are smaller than if you move the machine fast. You need to move the head at a consistent speed to keep the stitches the same size.

The learning curve for a non–stitch-regulated system will include learning how to maintain a steady speed of movement and learning the speed at which you are comfortable doing different designs. For example, you will probably want to use a faster stitch speed when doing a meander/stipple-type design than when you are stitching a more complicated one.

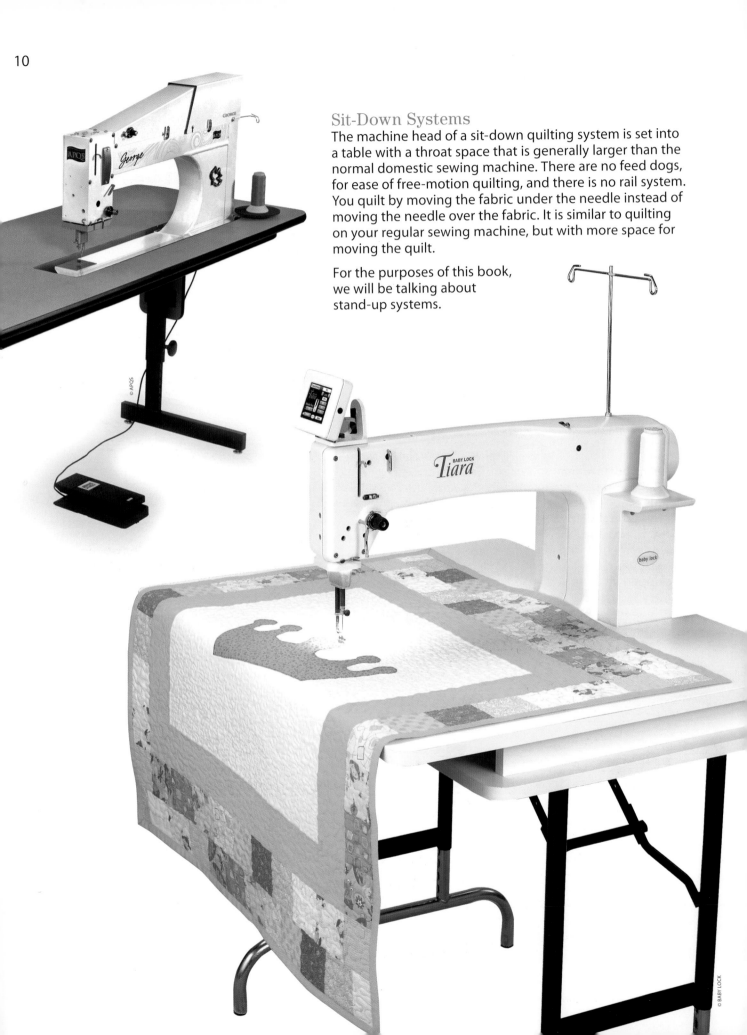

Sit-Down Systems

The machine head of a sit-down quilting system is set into a table with a throat space that is generally larger than the normal domestic sewing machine. There are no feed dogs, for ease of free-motion quilting, and there is no rail system. You quilt by moving the fabric under the needle instead of moving the needle over the fabric. It is similar to quilting on your regular sewing machine, but with more space for moving the quilt.

For the purposes of this book, we will be talking about stand-up systems.

Basic Parts of the Machine/Table

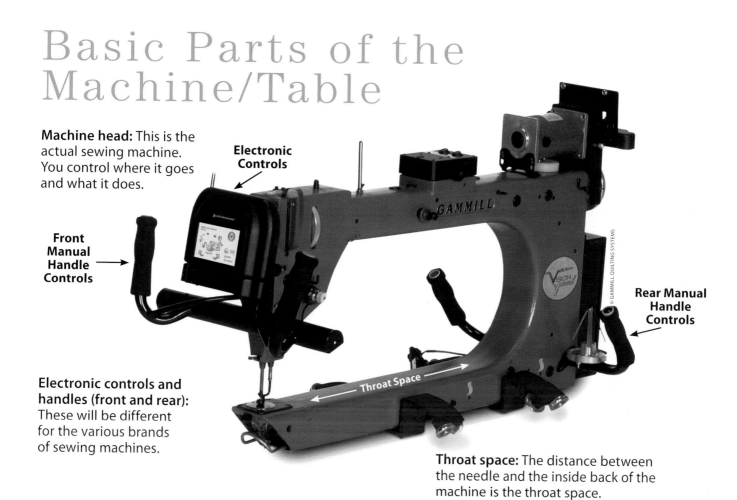

Machine head: This is the actual sewing machine. You control where it goes and what it does.

Electronic Controls

Front Manual Handle Controls

Rear Manual Handle Controls

Throat Space

© GAMMILL QUILTING SYSTEMS

Electronic controls and handles (front and rear): These will be different for the various brands of sewing machines.

Throat space: The distance between the needle and the inside back of the machine is the throat space.

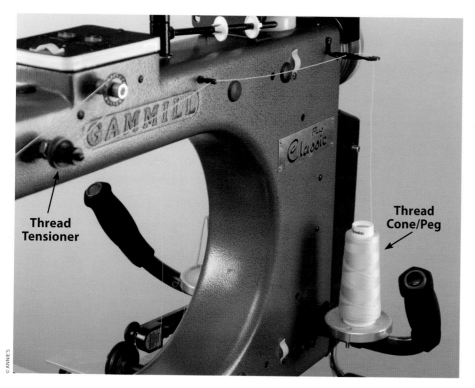

Thread Tensioner

Thread Cone/Peg

© ANNIE'S

Thread path with various tensioners: The path the thread takes from the cone to the needle through all of the tensioners. Each brand of machine will have a slightly different thread path. Refer to your manual for specific instructions.

Thread cone/spool peg: Mount where cone or spool of thread sits.

Hopping foot

Bobbin area

Needles

Wheels and track: Both vertical and horizontal wheels and track are shown.

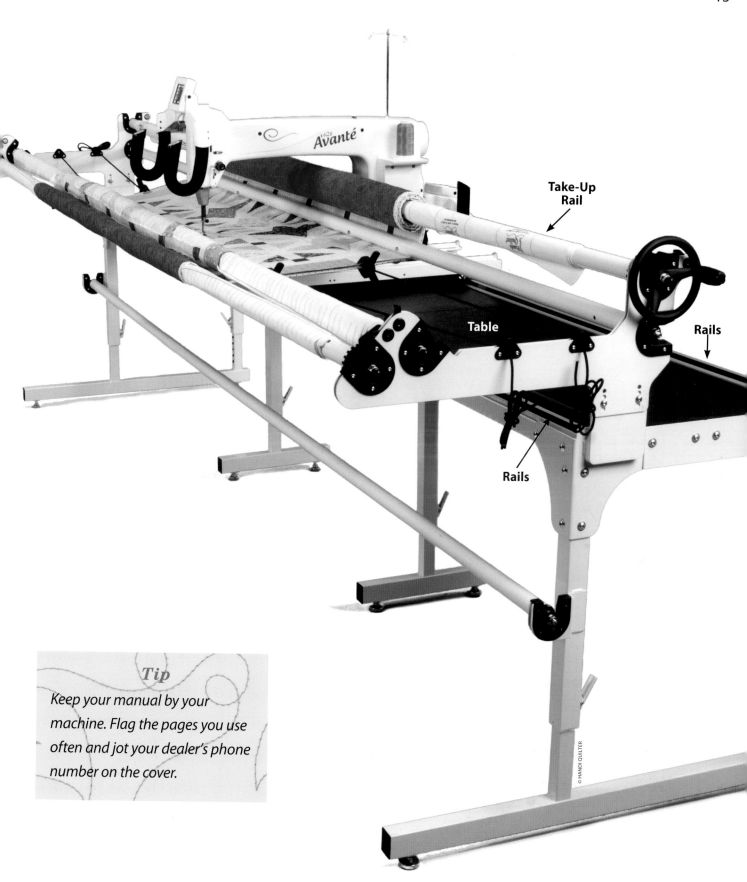

Take-Up Rail

Table

Rails

Rails

© HANDI QUILTER

Tip

Keep your manual by your machine. Flag the pages you use often and jot your dealer's phone number on the cover.

Supplies

About Thread

When we talk about quilting thread we have a different agenda than a discussion of piecing thread. Thread for piecing should blend into the seams so it is not visible. Quilting thread is the ink in your pen that creates the quilting design. It has color and presence. Thick, thin, variegated, contrasting or matching—thread makes a statement on a quilt. Ask yourself what kind of statement you want to make.

©THREAD TALES QUILTWORKS

Since the purpose of this book is to help you bond with your quilting system and to get you quilting, find a go-to thread that will run smoothly in your machine without breaks and shredding. Poly-wrapped, poly-core or long staple cotton threads are good choices. You do not need the frustration of thread issues while you are learning to use your quilting system.

Consult your machine dealer about the best machine-quilting threads for your system. Save specialty threads for later.

I have been fortunate to be able to run nearly any thread that is intended for high-speed machine

Tip

Cotton thread will produce more lint than polyester thread. When using cotton, be especially attentive to cleaning out your bobbin area where this lint tends to collect.

quilting without many issues. Check the thread label or manufacturer's website for this information. My go-to threads are poly-wrapped, poly-core Omni by Superior Threads and Permacore by A&E. These are strong and come in nearly 200 colors.

If you are a cotton purist, I suggest trying Signature 100 percent cotton thread for machine quilting from A&E or King Tut from Superior Threads. Both of these are long-staple cotton, which stand up to the speed and tension of most quilting systems.

Many longarm quilters use the same thread in the bobbin as they use on top. You may want to start out that way and then try other combinations.

Most of the time I use Bottom Line by Superior Threads for my bobbin. It is a 60-weight lint-free, filament polyester thread. Because it is fine (thin), I can wind much more thread onto my bobbins, cutting down on bobbin changes. It is available in 55 colors, so I can generally find a color that will coordinate well with, if not match, any top thread I am using.

These are just a few suggestions to get you started. I use many other threads that require a little bit of tension tweaking or changing to a different-size needle. These include metallic, silk and invisible. It is best to have some experience before venturing into using specialty threads.

Thread Color

As for colors, I suggest that you take a look at the quilt tops you have waiting to be quilted. If you generally make bright colorful tops, you are going to want to start your thread collection with some bright, colorful threads. If your tops tend toward Civil War, reproduction and traditional, then off-white, tan, khaki and sage green might be your best options.

About Batting

When choosing batting for a quilt my main considerations are—how will the quilt be used and what kind of look am I going for?

The 100 percent cotton battings tend to "read" flat—the quilting stitches don't show as much—while the blends provide more loft, allowing the quilting stitches to show.

©ANNIE'S

Some of the thinner cottons can be difficult to handle while loading the layers onto the machine. They can develop puckers and divots from your fingers as you are trying to load them. You can still use these thinner cotton battings, you just have to handle it with extra care.

You may have to do a little tugging and adjusting of the batting when you are advancing the quilt. A sturdy batting such as an 80/20 or 70/30 cotton/polyester blend will stand up to this treatment. An 80/20 batting (80 percent cotton, 20 percent polyester) is my go-to batting for strength and stability. Since I am primarily talking about practice pieces in this book I suggest a non-fussy, cotton/poly blend batting available from most major batting manufacturers.

When you are working with actual quilt tops you may want to consider the merits of other types of batting.

Make sure that the batting you choose is rated for machine quilting. This information can be found on the package or label, and on the manufacturer's website.

Types of Batting

Wool is lightweight and gives more loft and definition to the quilting designs. There are some terrific machine-washable and -dryable wools on the market now.

Polyester batting has more loft and is generally the least expensive option. It doesn't require special care before or after use. Polyester batting may beard—meaning little pieces of fiber may come through to the top of the quilt. If using a white batting with black or very dark fabrics, this bearding could show.

Extra high-loft polyesters are generally used for comforters and are usually tied rather than quilted. Your hopping foot may end up pushing your layers around if the batting is too thick.

About Needles

Most longarm machines use multidirectional needles. These needles are designed and made specifically for more accurate stitching when moving the machine in any direction. They are extra strong to allow maximum flexibility and bending. The deep scarf (where the thread lies) helps prevent thread breakage, skipped stitches and puckering. —*information found at www.superiorthreads.com*

Consult your dealer and/or manual about the specific needles for your machine.

Some quilters change their needle with each new project. In most cases, you can use them longer than that. I change mine when I begin to hear a ticking sound as the needle enters the quilt sandwich or if I cannot remember when I changed it last!

Your Owner's Manual

It is important that you read your owner's manual; keep it close by your quilting system. Many of the answers to your questions can be found there. In addition, you will find maintenance information such as cleaning, oiling, changing needles, etc. Write your dealer's phone number on the cover. Having a good relationship with your dealer can mean the difference between enjoying your quilting system and fighting with it.

Tip

Packaged batting made with natural fibers is often wrinkly and compacted from being stuffed into the package. You can get most of the wrinkles out and re-fluff the batting by spritzing it lightly with water and running it in the dryer on delicate for 10 minutes.

For polyester batting, draping it over the machine table overnight can help pull out some of the wrinkles.

Finding Your Comfort Zone

Spending quality time bonding with your quilting system means you should spend a few hours at a time standing and quilting. It is important to be comfortable. Here are a few things to consider when it comes to comfort and quilting.

Machine Height

The height of your quilting system is important. Many people are surprised by the height of my system table. It took a little trial and error to get it right.

If it is too low and you are hunching to get close to your work, you are tiring your back. If it is too high and you are reaching up too much, you are likely to end up with sore arms.

Since I work on my system several hours at a time, I need to be very aware of my body's position. Even at the very best height for me, I need to think about how I feel and do some stretching every so often. I confess that occasionally I get so involved in the quilting process that I forget to stretch and walk around until I get an achy reminder.

Flooring

Using a stand-up system means being on your feet. I was lucky enough to be able to create my studio from scratch by taking over and remodeling half of our basement.

I purchased tough industrial carpeting and the best pad for underneath it that I could find; this gave me a good cushion for heavy-duty wear and tear.

Adding industrial foam or rubber mats that run the length of your table is a good alternative when you are setting up a system in an already finished space.

Tip
Try to find mats with beveled edges. It helps to cut down on the possibility of tripping.

Wear comfortable shoes with good support. I can tell you from experience that when I forget to wear comfortable shoes I can feel it in my legs after just a couple of hours.

Heating & Cooling

Maintain a comfortable temperature and humidity level in your quilting space. It is difficult to concentrate on quilting if you are too hot or too cold.

Humidity can affect the quality of your quilting stitch. Too much humidity can make the fabrics, batting and thread "grabby" instead of "glide-y," leading to skipped stitches or breaking threads. Too little humidity can create static electricity that can interfere with the electronics of your system.

Tip
If your work area is very dry, always touch the table to discharge the static in your body before touching your machine head and turning it on.

Take Frequent Breaks

Trying to quilt when you are truly tired will magnify every tiny thing that isn't perfect. It is easy to become frustrated and cranky when tired. Have a good stretch and take a nap, or take a walk outside if you are not a napper. Come back to your machine later when you can enjoy it.

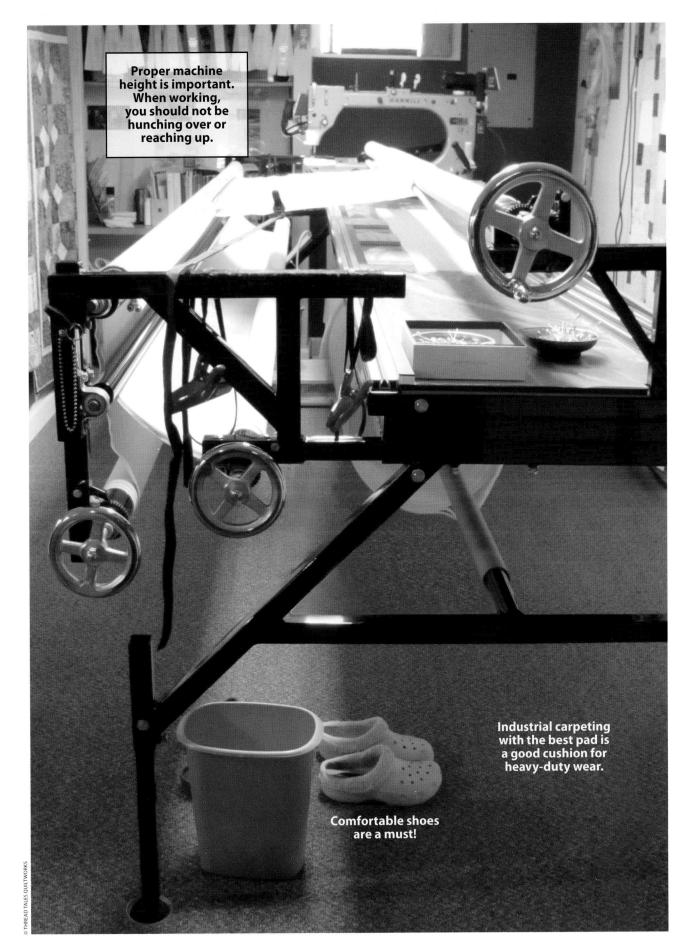

Proper machine height is important. When working, you should not be hunching over or reaching up.

Industrial carpeting with the best pad is a good cushion for heavy-duty wear.

Comfortable shoes are a must!

Practice, Practice, Practice

Drawing, Doodling & Otherwise Getting a Design Into Your Head

Please don't skip this very important step—doodling. Your machine head is like a giant pencil, and your needle is the lead. If you can create the design competently and consistently on paper, you will be able to recreate it more easily at the machine.

> ### *Tip*
> *I keep all of my drawing pads to flip through when I am looking for designs for a quilt.*

When you are contemplating a new design, your first task is to get the idea onto a dry-erase white-board or paper.

I have two sizes of dry-erase boards with different-color markers, and inexpensive newsprint pads with colored pens and pencils to doodle on. I generally start doodling a design on one of the dry-erase boards, trying to get a feel for the design without wasting paper. Then I transfer the design to the paper pads for a little more tweaking. Your first goal is to know where you are going and to be able to maintain consistency in the design's size, shape and density.

Your second goal is to be able to draw the design out without getting stuck in a corner or lost. Try to draw out your design without lifting your pen/pencil from the page/board. Simply pause and think—figure out where you are "stitching" next. Every time you lift your pen consider it a stop and start on a quilt.

Your third goal is to achieve an even density and/or consistency of size. You will get more consistent with practice. Pause every few minutes to see how well you are filling the space.

Practice Quilt Pieces

If you have decided to purchase a longarm quilting system you probably have a stack of quilt tops that you have been saving up, but set those aside for now. It is best to load a muslin quilt sandwich that you can play around on to get the feel of your system. You might also have to do some tweaking of your tension, and you don't want to be doing that on a real quilt if it can be avoided.

I confess that I loaded and re-loaded my first practice piece three times before I got it right. I had the manual open and followed it step by step—I still messed it up! By the time I loaded it successfully I was exhausted and had to take a break and get something to eat. It was not my best morning.

I recommend an inexpensive solid-color fabric like muslin, approximately 60" x 80" for the top and a 66" x 86" or 68" x 88" piece for the batting and backing. Your backing needs to be larger than the top to allow for pinning onto the leaders and clamping the sides. Use wide (90-inch) fabrics or piece regular-width fabrics to achieve the necessary size.

Please gather the following supplies for your practice piece.

- Muslin or solid-color fabric for top 60" x 80"
- Muslin or solid-color backing 66" x 86"–90"
- Two colors of thread that contrast with fabrics (one for the top and one for the bobbin—see About Thread on page 14)
- Batting 66" x 86" (I generally use an 80/20 cotton/poly blend—see About Batting on page 14)
- Small scissors for trimming threads (I use blunt-tip children's scissors at the machine. They help me avoid accidentally snipping fabric when I trim threads close to the quilt top.)
- Drawing pad and/or whiteboard
- Pen/pencil and/or dry-erase markers

PFAFF AND POWERQUILTER ARE TRADEMARKS OF KSIN LUXEMBOURG II, S.AR.L. ©2013 KSIN LUXEMBOURG II, S.AR.L.

Tip

My best piece of advice for beginning longarm quilters is to keep a practice piece on your machine. Whenever you do not have a quilt on your system, load a practice piece and keep it there until you are ready to load the next quilt. It makes it easy to spend some time on your quilting system every day. And spending that time every day will do more to build your skills and help you bond with your quilting system than anything else you can do.

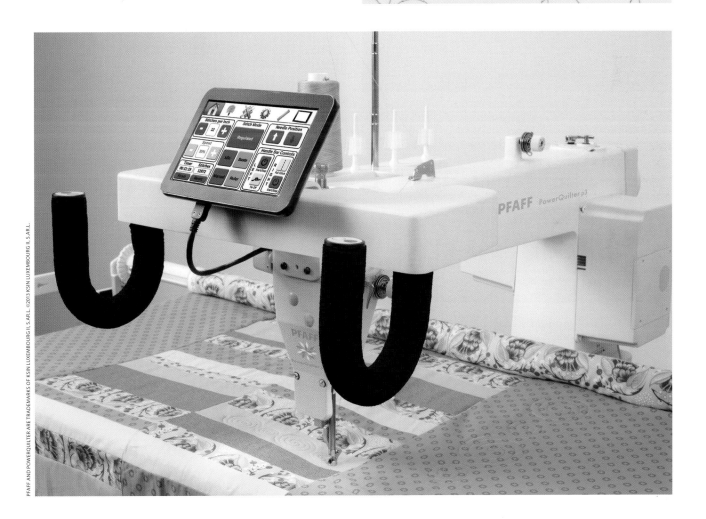

Attaching the Quilt to the Leaders (or Loading)

It is important that the quilt top and backing are centered on the frame. To accomplish this, clearly mark the center point on the take-up leader with a permanent marker.

Mark the other leaders by matching them up with the center mark on the take-up leader so that they align (see photo below).

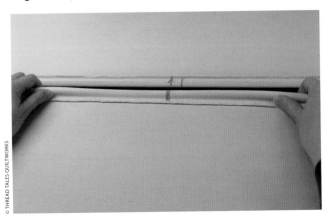

Centering the Top & Backing on the Leaders

Consult your manual for details on how to load the quilt layers on your particular machine.

To find the center of your top and backing, fold the edges that you intend to attach to the leaders in half. Mark the centers with a safety pin. Then align the safety pins with the center markings on your leaders.

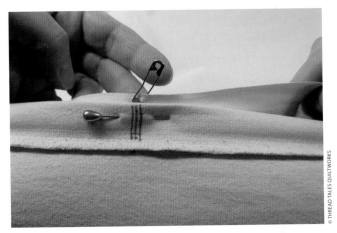

The three most common methods of attaching your quilt layers to the leaders are pinning, zipping and clamping.

Using Pins

Many longarm quilters start out by attaching the layers of the quilt to the leaders using extra-long sturdy pins.

Using pins is inexpensive, and it takes a little more time. I use this time to become friends with the quilt and think a little more about the quilting plan.

Pros—This method is inexpensive, simple and gives you Zen time with the quilt.

Cons—It is time-consuming and has the potential for bloodletting on to leaders or the quilt itself!

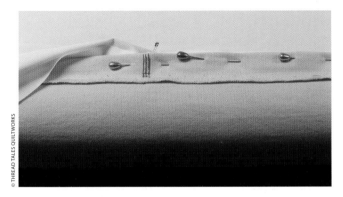

Tip

Wrap a piece of batting around the handle bar and use as a handy pincushion when pinning the layers to the leaders or when removing the quilt from the frame.

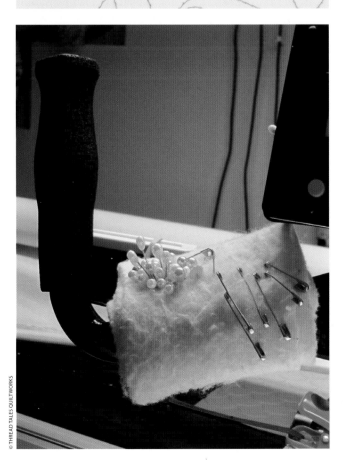

Tip

Pin in and then out and then back in to avoid catching clothes and pricking fingers.

Using Zippered Leaders

There are zipper systems available that allow you to zip the quilt backing and top onto and off of the leaders. This involves a little installation after purchase to attach one half of each set of zippers to each leader. Then you can either sit and pin or baste your quilt backing and top onto the other half of the zipper set.

Pros—You can sit and attach your layers to the free halves of the zippers. If you have more than one set of zippers you can take a partially quilted quilt off the quilting system to work on a different quilt for a while.

Zippers are especially nice if you are working on a labor-intensive show quilt and want a break to do work on something else for a little while.

Cons—Zipper leader systems are more expensive than pins and require a little up-front installation work.

Leader Snaps, Grips or Clamps

These loading systems work by sliding a stiff tube into the hem of your canvas leaders laying the edge of your backing (or top) onto the edge and clamping over them with long C-shaped tubes.

I use Red Snappers, pictured below, produced by Renae Haddadin of Quilts on the Corner.

Pros—Quicker loading of the quilt layers, seconds to unload and even tension across the entire width of the backing and top.

Cons—More expensive than pins and requires a small amount of up-front installation.

Stabilizing or Basting the Quilt

After you get the practice piece loaded, thread the machine, referring to your manual, with contrasting threads. The thread should not only contrast with the fabric, but the top and bobbin thread should contrast with each other. This will allow you to see each individual stitch and allow you to spot tension issues.

One of the joys of quilting on a longarm machine is that you do not have to baste your entire quilt sandwich before you begin to quilt.

I have recently learned that the conventional wisdom among many longarmers is to use "ABC" when loading the quilt sandwich: A—Attach to leaders, B—Baste, C—Clamp. However—I have always loaded ACB: A—Attach, C—Clamp, B—Baste. I didn't hear about ABC until I had been

Tip

You can use the horizontal channel lock or stop to check that the quilt is straight. Engage the horizontal lock at the upper left or right corner of your quilt top and move the machine head (without stitching) along the top edge of your quilt top.

longarming for a number of years. Yes, I have been doing it "wrong" for many years and continue to do so because it works for me. Try both methods and see which one best meets your needs.

Basting

After attaching the quilt to the leaders of the quilting system many quilters (including me) baste the quilt top to the batting and backing. Some longarm quilters use pins for this purpose, but most thread-baste using the machine.

I use the single-stitch option on my Gammill to baste approximately ¼" inside the raw edge of the top. I usually baste starting on the left-side edge at the lowest point my needle can reach, up the left side, across the top edge and down the right side as far as my needle can reach (Figure 1).

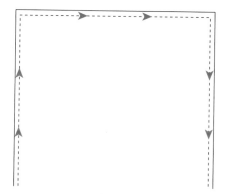

Figure 1

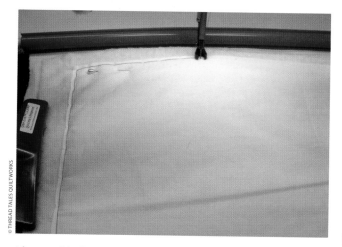

I have also heard of longarmers who baste across the quilt as close to the front rail as possible every time the quilt is advanced. I have not found this to be necessary, but I can see doing this with a particularly wonky quilt or a quilt sandwich that has a tendency to shift like a cotton/poly top with a poly batting.

Side Clamps

Side clamps help keep an even tension on the quilt sandwich from side to side, much like rolling the quilt onto the rails creates tension vertically.

Clamp only the backing and batting, which are larger than the quilt top for this reason. It is important not to put any extra stress on the quilt top in order to avoid distortion.

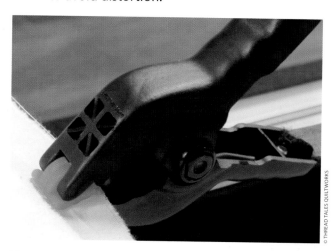

I have tried several kinds of side clamps. The ones that came with my Gammill, as shown above, are very strong and grip about an inch of fabric. They came in a set of four—two for each side. I was not 100 percent happy with them for two reasons. They are very stiff to open and since they grip only about 1" of the backing fabric, they create tension or "pull" in two very specific spots.

Two other types of side clamps on the market are Featherlight Clamps and Grip-Lite™ Side Clamps. Both brands have a wider gripping area, which creates a more even tension along the sides. They are also easier to open. I currently use the Grip-Lite clamps shown below and am very happy with them.

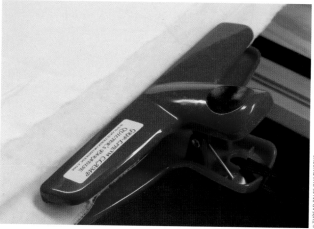

Quilt Sandwich Tension

Rolling the quilt sandwich onto the rails creates tension in the quilt itself, as does clamping the sides. I have found that many new longarmers want to tighten that quilt sandwich a little bit too much. The quilt should not be stretched to feel like a trampoline. You do not want to bounce a quarter on it!

Too much tension in the quilt can cause all sorts of problems. The most common are skipped stitches and broken/snapped needles.

As you move the machine head to create the quilting design the needle is going in and out of the fabric at a high rate of speed. This causes the needle to flex slightly in different directions. If there is too much tension in the quilt sandwich, even a strong multidirectional needle can flex a little too much causing the top thread to miss catching the bobbin thread creating a skipped stitch. Even worse, the needle can bend too far and snap.

You want a slight sag in the quilt sandwich. You should be able to poke a finger up from the bottom and grab it up to the first knuckle with your other hand.

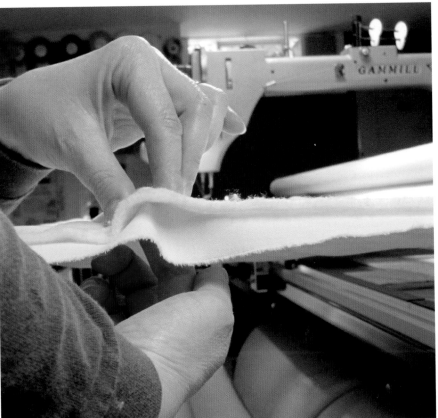

© THREAD TALES QUILTWORKS

> ## Tip
>
> *If you are getting skipped stitches, loosen your quilt sandwich a little bit and check to make sure your needle is inserted correctly before you move on to more complicated fixes.*

Quilting

Now that your quilt is loaded onto your system, you are ready to quilt.

Stops & Starts—Securing Your Stitches

You must secure the beginning and ends of your lines of stitching. Three common ways of doing this are: tiny stitches, back tacking, and knotting and burying.

Tiny Stitches

This is the method that I use most often to start and stop my lines of quilting. After I bring up the bobbin thread, I hold both threads securely in my left hand and take five or six tiny, tiny stitches (a couple of them backward) to lock in the stitches (Figure 2). This is easily done at the edge of the quilt where it will be hidden under the binding. It can often be hidden in a seam.

Figure 2

The designs you will learn in this book are allover or edge-to-edge designs. Securing your stitches in this way will be sufficient in this type of design.

Back Tacking

With this method, take three or four stitches forward and then go back, stitching on top of them (Figure 3). This is best used at the edge of the quilt, although it can be hidden in a seam if you are careful and your thread matches your fabric.

Figure 3

Knotting & Burying

I do occasionally knot and bury the thread tails if my bobbin runs out or if the thread breaks in a place on the quilt where another type of stop/start would be obvious. I keep a self-threading needle at my machine for this purpose.

To bring up the bobbin thread, take a couple of tiny stitches leaving a "tail" at the beginning of the line of stitching to go back to; knot and bury the tail inside the quilt sandwich much like for hand quilting (Figure 4).

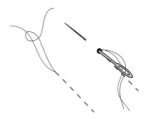

Figure 4

This method is a bit time consuming. I do not offer it in my longarm business. It is often used for show quilts. I do offer to leave tails for my clients to bury if they would like. There have been no takers so far!

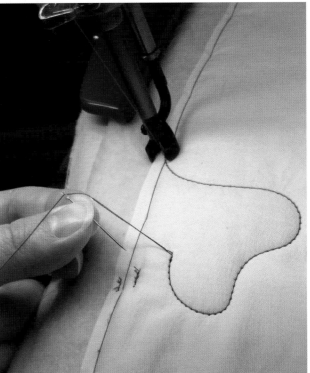

Ready to Quilt

Here we are. We have a lovely muslin sandwich loaded onto the quilt frame (not too tight!).

Contrasting thread is in the top and bobbin, and everything is nicely basted and ready to quilt.

Bring the machine head to the chosen starting point. Drop the needle and bring up the bobbin thread. Hold the top and bobbin threads firmly in your left hand.

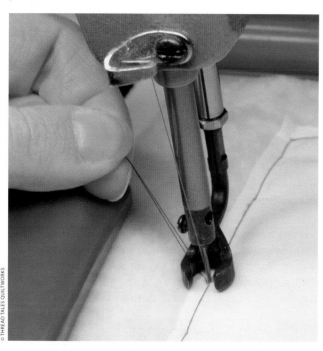

Make tiny stitches back and forth to lock in the line of quilting. Lay the tails away from the direction of the quilting.

Choose the speed (if not stitch-regulated) or engage your stitch regulator and begin moving the machine head, stitching in random directions. Make straight lines up and down, back and forth, wavy lines or loops and swirls. Get a feel for the machine.

Make sure you have a loose, comfortable grip on the handles. The machine head should move smoothly in all directions, and the stitches should look clean and regular. The goal here is to get a feel for the machine, not to make any particular design.

Stop every few minutes to take a good look at the stitches for tension and evenness. Reach under the quilt sandwich and run a fingernail over the stitching on the backing. It should feel smooth and should not make a ticking sound as your fingernail glides over the stitching.

The first time you pause in the stitching, go back and trim off the beginning thread tails. Get into the habit of trimming those right away. They can get wrapped around the hopping foot while you are quilting and cause all sorts of problems.

Beginning Glitches & Fixes

Correct or balanced thread tension means that stitches will appear on both sides of the quilt as shown in Figure 5.

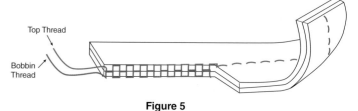

Figure 5

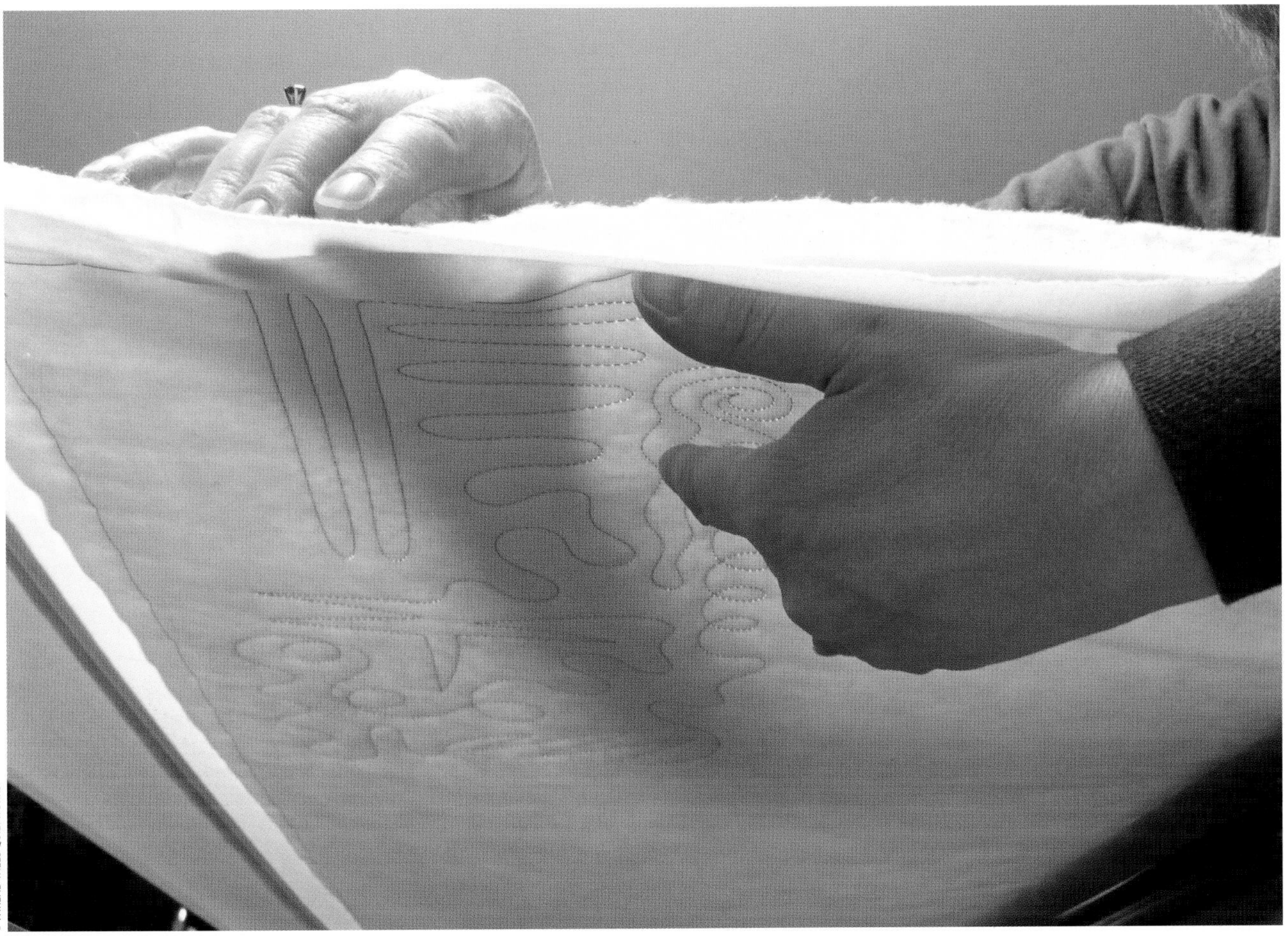

© THREAD TALES QUILTWORKS

Tip

Pay attention to your machine. The minute anything sounds or feels "off," stop and check your stitches on the quilt top and backing.

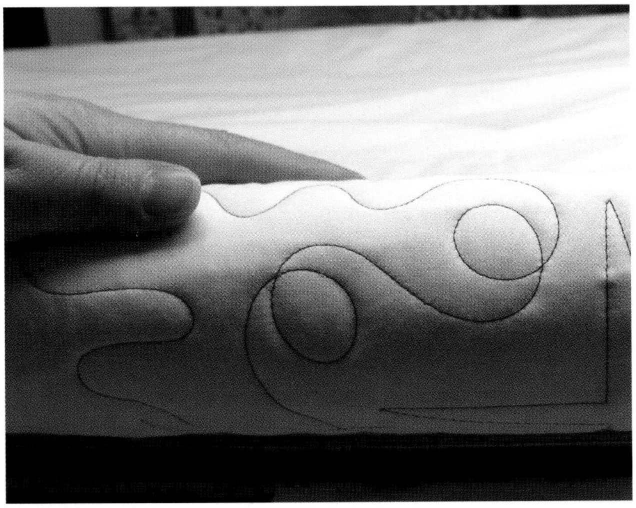

© THREAD TALES QUILTWORKS

If there are tension problems, such as flat stitching on the top or bottom of the quilt sandwich, or "pokies" (seeing the bobbin thread on the top of the quilt or the top thread on the bottom of the quilt), check your manual and make some slight adjustments. Remember, make small adjustments and then check the stitching. Continue to make small adjustments as needed.

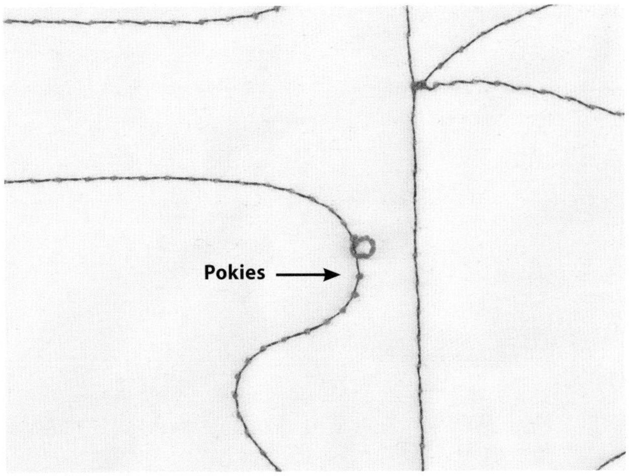

© ANNIE'S

Generally, if the top thread is lying flat on the quilt top, the top tension is too tight (Figure 6). Loosen it a quarter turn and see if that makes the difference.

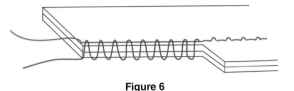

Figure 6

If the bobbin thread is lying flat on the backing, the bobbin tension is too tight (Figure 7). Loosen the bobbin tension.

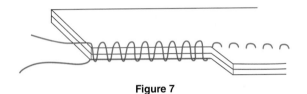

Figure 7

There are many things that can throw off your tension. Sometimes, the problem is the combination of fabric, batting and threads that make adjustments necessary. Sometimes, the thread has jumped out of one of the guides. Be patient and only change one thing at a time. Then stitch and check for improvement before you move on to another adjustment.

At this point, you are simply getting a feel for how your machine moves.

For issues such as difficulty moving in certain directions, vibration and wobbly areas, check your manual for possible solutions. If you are still having problems after trying everything that the manual suggests, you should call your dealer for more help.

When you can move your machine head freely, and you are feeling comfortable with the results, then move on to the next step.

> ### Tip
> If you are experiencing difficulty moving the machine after you have rolled the quilt, check that the take-up roller (the rail onto which you are rolling the quilt as you advance) is not resting on the bed of the machine causing "drag."

Developing the Freehand Design

For each design listed, you will learn how to:

• Control your machine
• Keep the density even
• Stitch smooth lines and curves
• Stop and start in the middle of a quilt when your bobbin runs out

For your convenience, there are Stitch Design Practice sheets beginning on page 48.

Basic Meander or Stipple

The meander or stipple is a terrific design element—it looks like a puzzle. Everyone's meander is just a little different—kind of like handwriting. This design is an excellent starting point for learning to look ahead and to practice keeping an even density.

I use the basic meander quite often in my quilting. I regularly use it on T-shirt quilts and busy, busy print quilts. It provides depth and texture without adding a competing design. It is also a very sturdy design for quilts that will be heavily used and frequently washed.

Doodle It

Drawing the meander on your whiteboard or large pad of paper will save you time when you go to the machine to stitch it out.

Cover the entire surface of the board/page. Repeat until you can cover the page evenly without drawing yourself into a corner. Remember, you can travel along an outside edge or backtrack to an open area if you need to. Every time you lift your pencil would be a stop and start if you were stitching.

> ### Tip
> *Draw out designs that are new to you. Doodle them until you are confident in your spacing and your path. This will make it easier when you take the design to the machine for the first time.*

Quilt It

Stitch, or draw a line across your practice piece using a permanent marker, approximately 10" down from the top edge. If you have a shortarm system, mark out this line as far down your piece as the throat space will allow.

Bring the machine head to the left side and drop the needle just outside the basting line. Bring up the bobbin thread and secure the stitches using your favorite method.

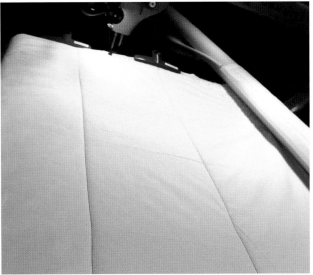

© THREAD TALES QUILTWORKS

© ANNIE'S

Basic Meander

Take a deep breath in and out. Loosen your grip on the handles, relax your shoulders, and start quilting. Remember that you have been drawing this design, so you should feel comfortable and know where you are going. Focus on keeping the density even throughout the pass, and try not to get stuck. Your goal is to make a medium-size meander with no more than an inch of space between the lines of quilting (Figure 8).

If you get lost or stuck, simply stop, pause and think for a second. Take a deep breath, loosen your grip, and start again. Your goal is smooth movement. Remember to breath and relax your shoulders and finish the pass.

Start

Figure 8

Tip

Do not watch the needle. It will go up and down in the quilt without you having to supervise it.

Do watch where you are going. You want to be looking ahead. Just like in driver's education when the instructor told you not to look at the nose of the car—look farther down the road.

Now, remove the side clamps and advance the quilt. Walk around to the back of the machine and run your hand under the freshly exposed backing to feel for waves or wrinkles. Now is the time to smooth out problem areas.

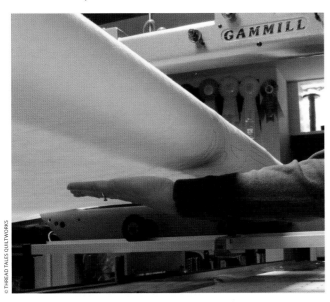

Look at the bobbin stitches on the take-up roller to see if there are any tension issues that you can't see from the top.

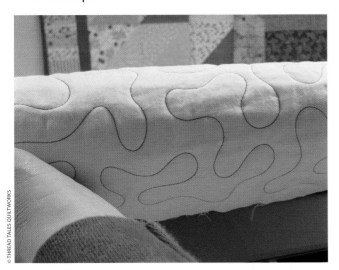

Return to the front of the machine and draw another line with about the same spacing as the first. Split this into two sections. In the first section make the meander smaller—no more than ½" between the lines of stitching. Keep your shoulders relaxed, your grip loose and breathe.

Try stitching a larger-size meander in the second section.

The meander should be feeling easier and the lines of stitching smoother. You should be getting lost or stuck less often.

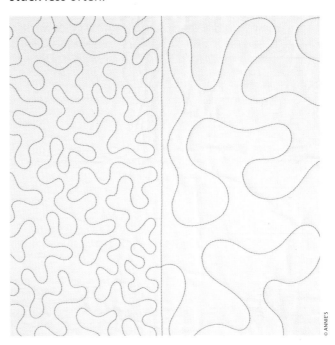

You can go over this same area until you are meandering evenly without getting lost. Change the thread color and go over it as often as it takes for you to feel comfortable enough to do this on a real quilt.

It may seem difficult at first to not follow the previous stitching, but this is good practice. Think of that previous stitching as a print fabric, which is what you will be quilting on soon!

Ribbon Meander

The ribbon meander is a large version of the basic meander that you are now already comfortable with. I have stitched this design on busy Christmas quilts using a shiny gold thread. Using a single color, variegated thread (example, light blue changing to dark blue) makes it look even more like a twisty ribbon.

Stitch a larger version of this pattern for an edge-to-edge, allover design, or stitch it small for a terrific background fill.

Doodle It

Draw out a meander on your drawing pad or whiteboard. When you have filled the page/board and come to a stop at the edge, do NOT lift the pen/marker. Draw backward along the original line ¼"–½" away, crossing at the bends in the design. Draw in this manner all the way back to the original starting point.

Do not be concerned about keeping the width between the two lines perfectly even. Redraw until you are happy with the look and density of the ribbon.

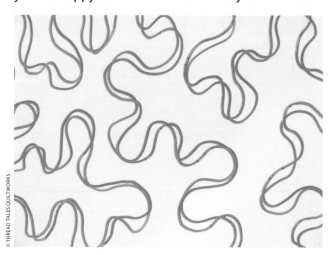

Quilt It

Advance the practice piece to the next unquilted section. Baste down the sides, step behind the machine, and run your hand under the quilt to check that the backing is smooth. Come back to the front and drop the needle in the left-side seam allowance. Bring up the bobbin thread and stitch another large (1" or 1½" in spacing) meander-stitch all the way across the section (Figure 9).

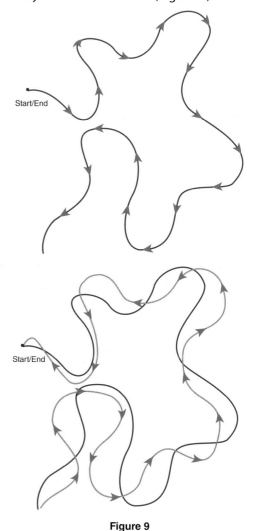

Figure 9

Tip

Check the backing of your quilt each time you advance the quilt. Walk around to the back of the table, check your bobbin stitches and run your hand underneath the quilt to check for possible wrinkles.

Ribbon Meander

When you get to the end, do not break the thread. Instead, quilt backward next to and crossing over the previous line of stitching referring again to Figure 9. Try to keep the new line of stitching approximately ¼"–½" away from the first line, except when crossing. I try to cross the lines where there is a bend in the design. Stitch all the way back to the beginning of the original line of stitching. The result should look like a twisty ribbon!

Loopy Meander

The loopy meander design is another good edge-to-edge, allover design. It is especially good for playful, colorful children's quilts. Quilted small, it makes a good background fill and can look like eyelet lace.

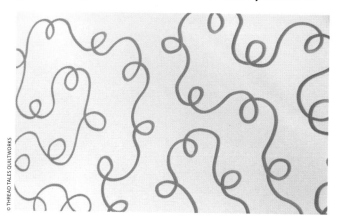

Adding other design elements, like leaves, changes the look as shown in the photo on page 34.

Unlike the basic meander when the general idea is not to cross the lines of stitching or have them touch, in the loopy meander we are deliberately crossing the line of stitching to create little loops.

Doodle It

When drawing out the design, soon you will notice that your loops tend to be about the same size. An "S" shape in between the loops is what helps change direction and enables you to fill up the space evenly (Figure 10). It may take a few pages of your pad or a few boards full of doodling to get the density even.

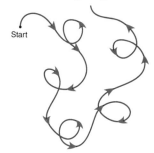

Start

Figure 10

When you are comfortable filling the space evenly without getting stuck you can take the design to the machine.

Loopy Meander

Loopy Meander With Leaves

Quilt It

Advance the practice piece to expose a new area on which to quilt. Don't forget to walk behind the machine and check the backing! Baste down both sides, and starting on the left edge, drop the needle and bring up the bobbin thread. Secure the stitches and begin stitching out the loopy meander. Do not worry if you get lost or stuck. Simply pause and think. Remember to breathe, relax your grip and your shoulders, and look where you are going, not where you have been.

By the time you have completed a full pass you should be comfortable. Compare the beginning of the stitching to the end of the stitch out—it should be smoother and have a more even density.

If you are not satisfied with your grasp of this design, change the thread color and stitch it out again right over the old stitching.

Tip

Is it time to change the needle?

If you are hearing a ticking or popping sound while you are stitching, or if you can't remember the last time you changed it, it is time to change your needle.

Wind/Water Meander

Quilted larger, the wind/water meander makes a great edge-to-edge design. Quilted small, it is perfect for background fills around snowmen, houses, fish, etc.

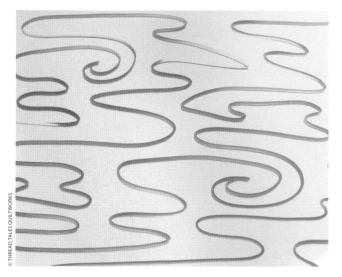

As with many abstract freehand designs, the wind/water meander takes its cue from the quilt that it is on. If you use this design around snowmen or trees it looks windy. Used around fish or water-color batiks it looks like water.

If you bring this design to a point rather than a smooth, curved end, it changes the feel and can even represent woodgrain or fire.

Doodle It

Grab your pad or whiteboard and draw this out. Essentially, you are doing an elongated meander. Drag the lines out horizontally and create an occasional swirl. Work back and forth across the surface until you fill up the space (Figure 11). Repeat on another sheet or wipe the board and do it again until you achieve an even density and are no longer getting lost or stuck in a corner.

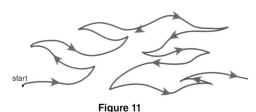

Figure 11

Quilt It

To practice a wind/water meander stitch out, advance the practice piece. Baste down the sides and mark off another pass. Drop the needle at the left side and bring up the bobbin thread. Secure the stitches.

Wind/Water Meander

Wind/Water Alternate Meander

Take a deep breath, loosen your grip and relax your shoulders. Begin stitching. Draw out the stitching lines working back and forth and up and down. If you get stuck, pause and evaluate where you need to go. Tie off and start again if you need to. Don't forget to add a swirl here and there.

Stitch half of the area. If you are feeling comfortable with your wind/water meander, then stitch the other half of the area with points. You want to stitch out a flattened "S" shape, point and "S" back.

Fit them into each other and fill the space. For woodgrain, add an occasional tight swirl in and out.

Repeat each design in a new thread color until you are comfortable enough to stitch this design on a real quilt top.

> ### *Tip*
> *Clean out your bobbin area thoroughly and often. I swipe it out whenever I change bobbins and do a thorough cleaning after each quilt.*

Filigree Meander

The filigree is a terrific design for feminine and floral quilt tops. Curvy and soft, it can be used in larger form as an effective edge-to-edge design or as a background fill when quilted smaller.

Like the loopy meander, it can be a little more difficult getting the right density. Even so, you may have to spend more time drawing than for some of the other designs.

This design is where you really start to work with a deliberate S shape. You are actually doing a lot of

S's in most of your designs so far, but here we use them to change the direction of the curlicue.

Doodle It

Begin drawing your practice sketches by curving up, over and down. Swoop into a circle shape and stop before closing it up. Backtrack around the circle nearly all the way and then "S" out to create a curlicue in the opposite direction (Figure 12).

Start

Figure 12

It can be a little difficult evenly filling the area. It may take a few pages to get the hang of it.

Quilt It

To stitch out a filigree design, mark off the next pass and divide the area in two. You will stitch this design larger to start with and smaller in the next area.

Baste down the sides. Drop the needle in the left seam allowance. Bring up the bobbin thread and secure the stitches.

As with the drawing, begin stitching by curving over, down and up.

Swoop into a circle shape and stop before closing it up. Backtrack around the circle nearly all the way and then "S" out to create a curlicue in the opposite direction. The lines are very close at the junction of the curling part and the line, and may even touch (Figure 13).

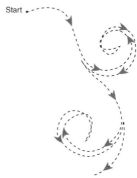

Start

Figure 13

Filgree Meander

I frequently add elements such as leaf or feather shapes to this design.

Tip

When backtracking around the curlicue, you do not need to track it perfectly. A little spacing between those stitching lines is charming.

Boxes Meander

The boxes design is very geometric. I use it on contemporary, masculine-style, retro and kitschy-type quilt tops.

Doodle It

To begin a box design, draw straight out, and then up, over, down, and as you close the box, draw over and through the first vertical line, up, back, close the box and draw through, changing direction again. This one takes a little more thought. Try for sharp corners. Catch part of one box in another. Make large and small sizes (Figure 14).

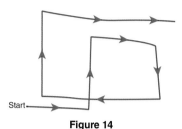

Figure 14

Rounding the corners changes the look of the design as shown on page 40. Do either all rounded or all sharp corners on a board/page of doodles until you can cover the whole area evenly without getting lost.

Quilt It

Mark off another pass (you can split this one in two if you'd like to do one with sharp corners and one with rounded corners). Baste down the sides. Drop the needle in the left seam allowance. Bring up the bobbin thread and secure the stitches.

Boxes Meander

Begin stitching out straight. Turn up, over, down and back over to cross the first vertical line and continue over and up to start a new box (Figure 15).

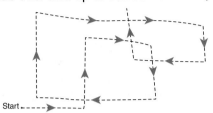

Figure 15

This is one you might want to stitch over in another color of thread. It may take a few attempts to be able to cover the area evenly.

Boxes Meander With Rounded Corners

© ANNIE'S

Quilting As a Business

There are enough considerations under this topic to fill another book, but let's touch on a few here.

Start-Up Costs
When considering the business of quilting for others, be aware that there are more start-up costs than the purchase of the quilting system. Licensing, insurance, supplies, education, tools and more add up quickly.

Time
Do you have the time in your life to run a small business? Do you work at an outside job, or do you still have small children at home? Be honest with yourself about how much time you can carve out of your life to start and maintain a business. It can and is being done by many professional quilters, but you may have to limit the number of quilts that you can take in.

Space/Location
Many professional quilters run their businesses from a studio in their homes.

Do you have the free space that the equipment will require? You need adequate room for the machine and enough room around it to be able to work, a large cutting table that doubles as a place to lay out clients' quilt tops for measuring and discussion at drop-off appointments, a large ironing surface for touching up tops and backings that develop creases from being folded, and a sewing table with your regular sewing machine installed. You also need room to store rolls or packages of batting should you decide to carry them as part of your business, room to safely store quilts waiting to be picked up, and tops/backings waiting to be quilted.

Do you have a separate entrance for your studio area or at least the ability to shut the door to the living spaces of your home?

If you are thinking of a separate location for your business, you need to factor in how much money you are going to have to earn to pay for or rent the location, pay property taxes, insurance, utilities, etc., before you can make a profit.

Physical Condition
I do not like to discourage anyone from this job, but do not kid yourself—this is a far more physical job than many people realize. Not only are you standing for most of your day, but folding, trimming and loading large pieces of fabric, and then unloading finished quilts requires bending, reaching and stretching—a lot of it.

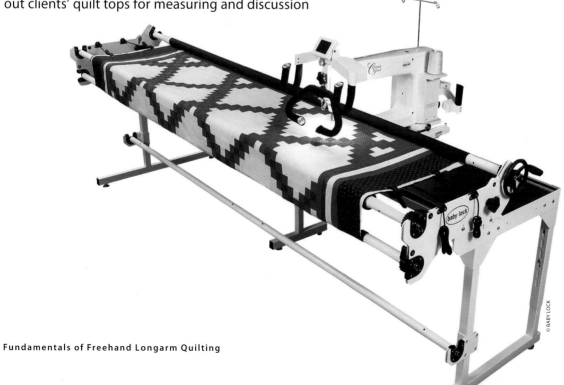

© BABY LOCK

Work Personality

Be very honest with yourself about your ability to work at home. Are you easily distracted? Will you get into the studio and quilt when it is a nice day when you would rather take the kids to the park or work in the garden instead?

Are you organized not only in your quilting area, but also with paperwork? Do you manage your time well?

Professionalism

I personally believe a dedicated phone number for your business is critical. I use my cellphone for this purpose. I answer the phone by saying "ThreadTales Quiltworks, Terri speaking." This is the first contact many of my clients have with me, and I want them to know they are going to be working with a professional.

Appointments

Making drop-off and pick-up appointments for specific times helps keep the drop-bys to a minimum. If you treat your schedule casually, your clients will treat it casually as well.

Paperwork

Work orders, invoices, receipts—paperwork is boring, but important. I write out a work-order form while I am with the client at the drop-off appointment. It has a carbonless duplicate. After the client signs it, they get a copy. That way the client has a copy of what we discussed, a firm date of when the quilt will be finished, and the cost.

Pricing

Pricing is a difficult process. There are many different ways that professional quilters figure their pricing. Some choices are: by the square inch, square foot, square yard, by the hour, and by the general size (twin, full, etc.). You will have to choose the method that makes the most sense to you.

Stress

Quilting is such a relaxing activity, isn't it? The colors, the fabrics, the pretty threads …

Quilting as a business is a little different. You still have the fabrics and the pretty threads, but now you are taking someone else's project

(a project that they may have spent a lot of time and money on already) and throwing it on the rack and punching a couple of hundred thousand holes in it.

How will you handle it if they are not happy? It may not have anything to do with your work, but you still have to deal with this unhappy client in a way that will satisfy you both.

Research

Do your research. How far out are the longarmers in your area booked? Two weeks? Three months? Or more? Is there room in the market for another quilter?

Is there something different that you could offer? Are most of the longarmers in your area custom quilters? Maybe you want to develop less expensive allover designs as your specialty.

Groups

See if there is a longarm group that you can join in your area. You can learn so much from these groups and see different ways that they handle business.

Like everything else in life, there is no one right way. But there is a way that can work for you.

Do your research. Be honest with yourself about the time, money and space you have to invest, and you can have a successful professional quilting business. ∎

Resource Guide

This list of resources is meant to be used as a guide to locate more information and places to purchase product for your longarm use. All efforts have been made to ensure that the information given is correct. Both wholesale and retail sites are included.

Forums, Chat Groups & General Information

www.quiltwithus.connectingthreads.com/
   group/longarmquilters/

www.quiltingboard.com

www.creativelongarmquilting.blogspot.com

www.quiltscomplete.com

www.quiltingcreations.com

www.sharonschamber.com

www.brewersewing.com

www.willowleafstudio.com

www.quilttech.com

www.annebright.com

www.longarmsupplies.net

www.houseofhansen.com

www.longarmchat.com

www.a1quiltingmachines.com/forum
   (mostly for A1 machines)

www.mqresource.com/forum

www.groups.yahoo.com/group/
   Machine_Quilting_Professional/

Batting

Airtex
   www.airtex.com

Bosal
   www.bosalonline.com

Fairfield
   www.fairfieldworld.com

Hobbs Bonded Fibers
   www.hobbsbondedfibers.com

Matilda's Own Batting
   www.matildasown.com

Mountain Mist
   www.mountainmistlp.com

Pellon
   www.shoppellon.com

Quilters Dream Batting
   www.quiltersdreambatting.com

The Warm Company
   www.warmcompany.com

Gadgets & Tools

Annie's Quilt & Sew
AnniesCatalog.com

By Design Quilting LLC
www.patbarryquilts.com

Circle Lord
www.loriclesquilting.com

Constantine Quilts
www.constantinequilts.com

Creative Grids
www.creativegridsusa.com

DeLoa's Quilt Shop
www.deloasquiltshop.com

The Gadget Girls
www.thegadgetgirls.com

The Grace Company
www.graceframe.com

Kimmy Quilt
www.kimmyquilt.com

King's Men Quilting Supply Inc.
www.kmquiltingsupply.com

Lakeside Quilt Company
www.lovetoquilt.com

Leader Grips
www.leadergrips.com

Longarm Supplies
www.canadianlongarm
supplies.com

Quilt-EZ
www.quilt-ez.com

Quilter's Rule
www.quiltersrule.com

Quilts on the Corner—Red Snappers
www.renaequilts.com

Runway Ranch LAQS
www.sewfarsewgood.org

Machine Manufacturers

A1 Quilting Machines
www.a1quiltingmachines.com

ABM International (Innova)
www.abminternational.com

American Professional Quilting Systems (APQS)
www.apqs.com

Artistic Quilter 18
www.artisticquilter18.com

Baby Lock
www.babylock.com

Bailey's Home Quilter
www.baileyssewingcenter.com

Consew
www.carusew.com

Gammill Quilting Systems
www.gammill.net

Handi Quilter
www.handiquilter.com

Hinterberg Design
www.hinterberg.com

Homesteader
www.thequiltingsolution.com

JUKI America Inc.
www.jukihome.com

Martelli Enterprises
www.martellinotions.com/
longarm.asp

Nolting Mfg.
www.nolting.com

Pennywinkle Valley Ranch
www.pennywinklevalley
ranch.com

Pfaff
www.pfaffusa.com

Prodigy Machine Corporation
www.prodigyquilter.com

TinLizzie
www.tinlizzie18.com

Supplies

**BackSide Fabrics
(wide fabric for backings)**
www.backsidefabrics.com

Brewer Quilting & Sewing Supplies
www.brewersewing.com

**Christian Lane Quilters
(wide fabric for backings)**
www.christianlanequilters.com

Columbia River Quilting & Designs
www.columbiariverquilting.com

Constantine Quilts
www.constantinequilts.com

King's Men Quilting Supply Inc.
www.kmquiltingsupply.com

Linda's Electric Quilters LLC
www.lequilters.com

Longarm University
www.longarmuniversity.com

The Quilted Rose
www.thequiltedrose.com

Texas Quilt Machines
www.quiltfrog.com

Urban Elementz
www.urbanelementz.com

Thread Manufacturers

American & Efird (A&E)—Signature
www.amefird.com

Coats & Clark
www.coatsandclark.com

DMC
www.dmc-usa.com

Fil-Tec
www.fil-tec.com

Gutermann
www.gutermann-thread.com

Melco
www.melcousa.com

Presencia
www.presenciausa.com

Robison-Anton
www.robison-anton.com

Sulky
www.sulky.com

Superior Threads
www.superiorthreads.com

WonderFil
www.wonderfil.net

YLI Corp.
www.ylicorp.com

Thread Retail

Cranberry Quiltworks
www.cranberryquiltworks.com

Golden Threads
www.goldenthreads.com

King's Men Quilting Supply Inc.
www.kmquiltingsupply.com

Linda's Electric Quilters LLC
www.lequilters.com

The Quilted Rose
www.thequiltedrose.com

Southern Thread Inc.
www.southernthread.com

Superior Threads
www.superiorthreads.com

Texas Quilt Machines
www.quiltfrog.com

© THE GRACE COMPANY

Glossary of Terms, Slang & Otherwise Confusing Longarm Words

Like participants in any other activity, longarm quilters have developed terms that may need some explanation. Some of these words will be familiar from other sewing activities.

Background Fill

Designs quilted small and tight in backgrounds of appliqué or pieced blocks to "pop" the foreground.

Backtracking

Stitching over a previous line of stitching to travel to a new area.

Bird's Nest

A tangled wad of thread usually found on the backing and most often at starts and stops.

CC

Continuous curve designs. CC designs use the seam lines and intersections to create a quilting design that limits starts and stops within the quilt.

Custom Quilting
Two or more separate designs used when quilting a quilt.

DWR
Double Wedding Ring quilt.

Extended Throat Plate/Extended Base
A removable platform added to the needle end of the bed of the machine to give added support for using rulers and templates.

Floating the Top
A method of loading the quilt top onto the machine. The top is basted to the batting and backing and allowed to hang down the front of the table without being attached to the quilt top leader.

Freehand
Quilting a design without following a paper pattern or using a computer to control the machine.

Friendly Borders
Borders that ripple along the edges instead of laying flat.

Frogging
The painful process of removing quilting stitches, as in "rip-it, rip-it." Ten minutes of quilting can mean an hour or more of frogging.

Fullness
Extra fabric either within the body of the quilt or in the borders that causes puffed-up areas.

GMFG
Grandmother's Flower Garden pattern.

Panto, Edge to Edge, E2E, Allover
Freehand, paper or computerized designs that are generally quilted across the quilt without regard to piecing, appliqué or borders.

Partial Float
A method of loading the quilt top onto the machine. The bottom edge of the quilt top is pinned or clamped to the quilt top leader, and the top edge is brought up and basted to the batting and backing.

Pokies
Dots of bobbin thread showing on the top of the quilt or dots of top thread showing on the backing.

Railroad Tracks
Small loops of top thread showing on the backing or small loops of bobbin thread showing on the top of the quilt.

Ruler Work
Using acrylic templates and rulers held on the quilt top to guide the machine. Most, if not all, machines require the addition of an extended throat plate or extended base to be installed before using rulers.

Scrim
A loosely woven polyester net that is within the batting to secure fibers and provide stability.

SID
Stitch in the ditch.

Stipple, Meander, Puzzle Meander
Stipple and meander are often used interchangeably to indicate a wandering, curvy stitching line that does not cross itself. The correct usage of a meander is a larger allover design and a stipple is a small background fill.

TT
Terry Twist. A specific type of continuous curve design named for Sally Terry.

Wonky
A crooked top or backing.

YBR
Yellow Brick Road quilt.

Stitch Design Paths

End

Basic Meander

Start

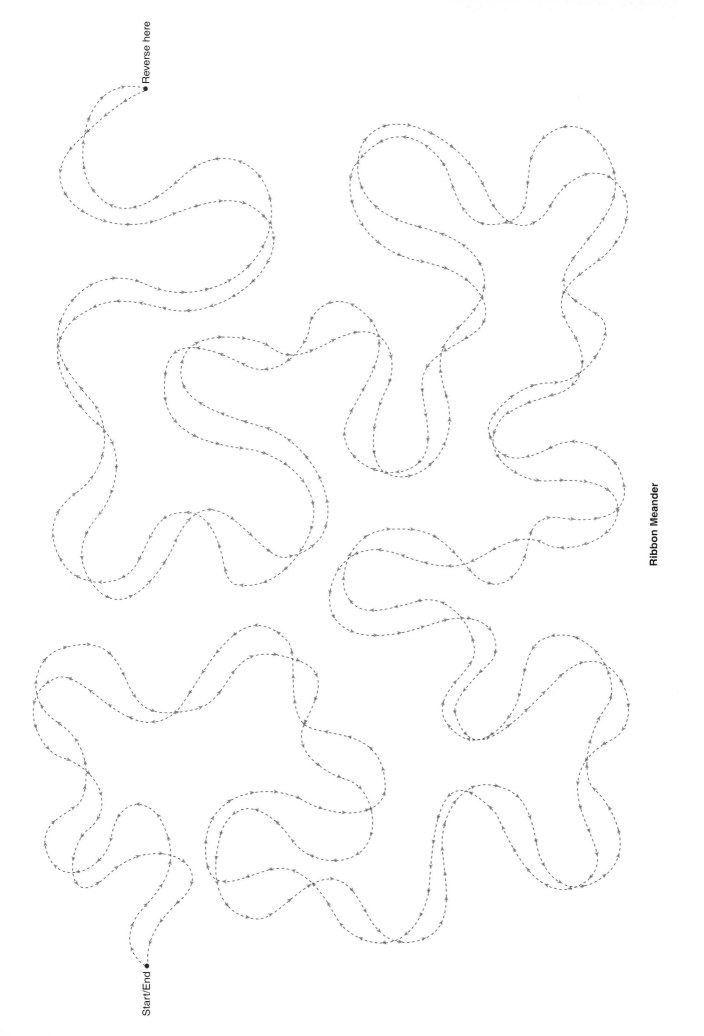

Start/End

Reverse here

Ribbon Meander

Loopy Meander

Start

End

Wind/Water Meander

End

Start

Wind/Water Alternate Meander

Filigree Meander

Start •

• End

Boxes Meander

End

Start

Notes

Special Thanks

We would like to thank the following manufacturers and businesses for their support in providing products and images for this publication.

American & Efird LLC
www.amefird.com

APQS
www.apqs.com

Baby Lock
www.babylock.com

Gammill Quilting Systems
www.gammill.com

The Grace Company
www.graceframe.com

Handi Quilter
www.handiquilter.com

JUKI America Inc.
www.jukihome.com

Masterpiece Quilting, Berne, Ind.

Nolting Mfg.
www.nolting.com

Pfaff
www.pfaffusa.com

Quilts on the Corner
www.quiltsonthecorner.com

ThreadTales Quiltworks, Grandville, Mich.

TinLizzie
www.tinlizzie18.com

YLI Corp.
www.ylicorp.com

Fundamentals of Freehand Longarm Quilting is published by Annie's, 306 East Parr Road, Berne, IN 46711. Printed in USA. Copyright © 2013 Annie's. All rights reserved. This publication may not be reproduced in part or in whole without written permission from the publisher.

RETAIL STORES: If you would like to carry this book or any other Annie's publication, visit AnniesWSL.com.

Every effort has been made to ensure that the instructions in this book are complete and accurate. We cannot, however, take responsibility for human error, typographical mistakes or variations in individual work. Please visit AnniesCustomerCare.com to check for pattern updates.

STAFF

Editor: Carolyn S. Vagts
Creative Director: Brad Snow
Publishing Services Director: Brenda Gallmeyer
Managing Editor: Barb Sprunger
Graphic Designer: Nick Pierce
Copy Supervisor: Corene Painter
Senior Copy Editor: Emily Carter
Copy Editor: Mary O'Donnell
Technical Editors: Angie Buckles, Sandra Hatch

Production Artist Supervisor: Erin Brandt
Senior Production Artist: Nicole Gage
Production Artists: Glenda Chamberlain, Edith Teegarden
Photography Supervisor: Tammy Christian
Photography: Matthew Owen
Photo Stylists: Tammy Liechty, Tammy Steiner

ISBN: 978-1-59635-621-4
123456789